Angel Arise

A. H. SCHWARTZ

PAGE PUBLISHING, INC.
Conneaut Lake, PA

First originally published by
Page Publishing 2021

ISBN 978-1-6624-4170-7 (pbk)
ISBN 978-1-6624-4171-4 (digital)

Printed in the United States of America

Chapter 1

Nancy was an only child whose parents died in a car accident when she was seven. With no relatives around, Nancy ended up in foster care. She bounced around from house to house until she was sixteen and ran away. She ended up on the streets, broke and afraid. She couldn't find a job and needed money to live. She ended up selling her soul to the devil in the arms of men to survive.

Tony grew up in a bad part of town with a single mom who worked two jobs. When his mother got laid off, he knew he had to find a way to make money to help support the family. He was an influential twelve-year-old who fell into the wrong crowd. He started doing favors for the local gang to make ends meet. Within a few years, he made his way up the ladder and had his own corner to sell on.

One cold February night, they both got picked up and met at the local precinct. It was love at first sight. They started working on the same corner. A few months later, Tony asked Nancy to come to his mom's house for Sunday dinner. She was unsure at first but finally agreed. She was so happy that she went. His mother imminently made her feel welcome. She hasn't felt that happy or loved in a long time. A week later, at Sunday dinner, Tony asked Nancy to marry him. She, of course, said yes. She finally had a family. They started saving everything they had to buy a house. They even talked about going back and finishing school. They were heading on a path to success, but their plans were shattered when Tony's mother suddenly died. She had made no final preparations, so they had to pay for her funeral out of their savings. Her house was taken by the bank. The rest of their money was spent on a plane ticket for Tony's sister to live with their aunt two states away. After they dropped his sister off at the airport, they went to a local diner for breakfast.

As they were sitting there, trying to figure out what they were going to do next, Nancy took Tony's hand and said, "What are we going to do for us?"

He said, "What you mean?"

She looked at her stomach and said, "We are a family."

They both started crying.

On a warm summer night, a baby was born in a cardboard box in a back alley—a beautiful little girl with sparkling blue eyes and fair skin. She was given the name Jewel. Her parents didn't have anything to offer her but love, but she didn't need anything more.

Jewel didn't grow up like a normal child. She didn't have a nice cozy bed to sleep in every night or parents that worked normal nine-to-five jobs. Her mother was a prostitute, and her father a drug dealer, but she did not see them that way. They were just two people who loved her and would do anything for her. They would get food from the local food bank and made a house with washer and dryer boxes.

Chapter 2

When Jewel's mother was out turning tricks, her father would take her to the convenience store in front of the corner when he conducted his business.

The cashier was a widowed older woman who never had kids. She set up a playpen behind the register. She would watch Jewel while her father worked. When he was done for the night, he would give the cashier twenty dollars and take Jewel home.

A year after Jewel was born, a rookie cop named Officer Bridges started working on their block. He was tall with green eyes and brown hair. He had a long beard that Jewel liked to put her fingers in. He knew her parents were criminals, but he took pity on the innocent child. He was married with twin daughters that are seven months older than Jewel. Their names were Maddy and Lily. They had the same green eyes as their father. He became close to the family and would give them his daughter's hand-me-downs. He even had her over for sleepovers on really cold nights. They became family to her. The three girls were like sisters. They were potty trained together, went shopping for matching outfits, and even learned to ride bikes together. She knew she could go to Officer Bridges for anything. His wife was a lawyer and would represent her parents whenever they would get busted. She would do her best to get the charges dropped or community service.

Jewel's father had a regular client who was an ER nurse. She would buy pot from him to relax after a long shift. Her name was Stephanie. She was short with curly red hair. She was single and lived in a tiny one-bedroom apartment with her two cats.

Steph would give them medicine when Jewel would have minor coughs and colds. Also, she would clean up Nancy when her johns would get a little rough with her. When she wasn't working, she would take Jewel to play with her cats and knit them hats and blankets to keep warm in the winter. Jewel may not have any blood family around expect her parents, but she was definitely loved and taken care of.

Chapter 3

At age five, her parents put on their best clothes and enrolled her in school. They did not have a house, so they put down the address of the abandoned building in front of the alley where they lived. Her parents made sure she knew how important school was. Officer Bridges's wife would pick her up for school every morning since she went to the same school as the twins. She would always have a packed lunch for her. Jewel's mother would help her with her homework every night before she went out. There was a local gym down the street where they would shower. Jewel was very outgoing and made lots of friends. She loved going to play dates and birthday parties. Her parents always made sure she had a gift and minded her manners. Her parents did their best to make sure no one at school knew anything about her home life. They couldn't even imagine CPS finding out about her and taking her away.

As Jewel got older, she realized that she wasn't normal. She would go to her friend's house and see all of their nice things. But then their parents would get home from work, all tired and stressed out, and complain about their day at work. They would be so preoccupied with everything else that sometimes they wouldn't even say hi to their kids when they walked in the door. She would see her friends' parents worried about bills and making sure they had the latest fashion in clothes and furniture to impress their friends. They would get upset with their kids if they didn't do their chores or got a bad grade on a test. That's when Jewel realized that she had a pretty good life after all. Her parents may not be rich and have nice things, but they were happy, relaxed, and always had time for her. She knew, without a doubt, that they loved her and would do anything for her.

Jewel did pretty good in school but was having a little trouble in math. So when Jewel got older, her dad would take her to the corner to make a change for his customers. Most of them were friendly about it, but some would get annoyed. One night, a customer came and was in a hurry and didn't want Jewel to figure out his change. He got mad and started yelling at Tony and pushed Jewel on the sidewalk. She scraped her knee. Tony got mad and started shoving the man. Jewel was scared and ran in the store. The cashier calmed her down with a Band-Aid and a lollipop. When the man got in his car and left, Tony came into the store to check on her. Tony explained that not everyone in the world was nice. That some were mean because they were spoiled, others because of something going on at home, and others just because they can be. He told her that no matter what people say to her or how they look at her to hold her head up high and be proud of herself. That she knows that she has a family that loves her and stands behind her no matter what. Even at the young age of ten, she understood what her father was saying. Tony decided to leave the corner earlier that night and take Jewel to get some ice cream. When Nancy got home later that night, Tony told her what happened. Nancy feared for their little girl—about the way people would treat her because of her home, the way she would be judged because of her parents' job, and the example they were setting for her. Raising her around crime and the people they associated with. No one got much sleep that night.

Chapter 4

The next day was the twins' birthday. They were having a big party with all their friends. When Officer Bridges picked her up, he noticed the Band-Aid on her knee and asked what happened. She told him about the fight the night before and told him what her father said. He said that he agreed with what her father said and that it was his job to put bad people in jail to keep the good people safe. Jewel was confused because she had seen other cops arresting her parents. Officer Bridges explained that her parents themselves weren't bad but that their jobs were against the law, so they had to be punished. Just like when she is bad, she has to sit in time-out. Jewel had never realized that her parents' jobs were illegal. When they arrived at the house, he told her not to worry about it and enjoy the party.

At the party was Amy Brown, the most popular girl in school. Her father was a wealthy businessman who catered to her every whim. Her mother died during childbirth, and she uses that every chance she gets to get out of trouble or if she wants a new toy. Amy liked the twins but not Jewel. She asked Jewel why she was always with the twins as if she was some kind of pet or charity case. She made fun of her clothes and the gift she brought. Then she tried to get the twins to play outside with her without Jewel. The twins said no, and the four girls got in a fight. Their mom broke up the fight and called Amy's dad to come pick her up.

Later that night, when Officer Bridges was driving her home, she asked him if she was a charity case like what Amy said. He said no; that he loves her like family and never saw her that way. He said that he loves helping people, and that is why he became a cop. Then he reminded her that she can come to him for anything, that she is just like his daughters, and that she should never feel like a burden. He pulled up in front of her alley and kissed her on the forehead, and she got out of the car.

When Jewel's parents got home that night, she couldn't stop thinking about what Officer Bridges said about their jobs. She asked them, and they said yes. They explained how neither of them finished high school or went to college, so it was hard for them to get real jobs. They said that is why they are so hard on her about school. She asked them why they never went back and finished. They said they would look into it. The next Monday at school, Amy walked into class and announced that she was moving to China for a new business deal her dad got. The next week, the class had a going-away party for her. They never heard from her again.

Chapter 5

A few months later, school let out for the summer. Jewel's parents decided to enroll in summer school to get their GED. Jewel was so happy and made sure they did their homework every night like they did to her. Steph would watch Jewel so they could study and even helped make flash cards. September arrived, and it was the day of the big test. Jewel wished them good luck and went to class as they headed to the gym to take the test. A few hours later, they met Jewel in the cafeteria where she was eating lunch.

They both said they thought they did good but would have to wait to get their scores in the mail. Jewel had a spelling test that day and got a ninety-five on it. After school, they grabbed some pizza to celebrate.

The next two weeks felt like years waiting for their scores to come in. Finally, one day after school, Jewel checked the mail, and they were in. She ran as fast as she could through the alley to give them their scores. Tony opened his first. He passed with an eighty-five. He was so happy. Next, Nancy opened hers. She failed by two points. It was devastating. Tony told her not to give up and that she could retake it again next month and that he would help her study every night. They are a family, and no one gets left behind. She studied extra hard for the whole month and passed with a seventy-nine. Mr. and Mrs. Bridges threw them a small graduation party and helped them apply for jobs. They started applying everywhere they could—gas stations, convenience stores, and grocery stores. It took a while to get someone to hire them with their records, but Tony finally got a job as an overnight stocker and Nancy as a waitress. Tony stopped selling drugs. He referred his customers to a friend who sold. His customers understood. They were happy to see him turning his life around and trying to make a better future for his family. Nancy's customers, on the other hand, weren't as understanding. She stayed with her regulars for a few months until she found the right girl for each one's likes and needs. Things were starting to look up for the family. Now that they had real jobs, they could apply for public assistants and even saved up enough for a two-bedroom apartment in Stephanie's building.

Chapter 6

It was a cold December day when they moved into the apartment. Jewel was so excited she had all her clothes and toys packed in a kitty cat suitcase that the twins gave her. The Bridges even bought them a pot and pan set as a housewarming gift. Stephanie bought curtains, towels, and washcloths. They moved all of their belongings in, then went to the grocery store and filled the cart with food. Jewel was so happy to help pick out stuff for lunch and help plan dinners. They went home and put away all the groceries. Nancy tried to cook dinner, but it has been so long since she cooked that she burnt it. They ordered a pizza and bought a cookbook.

Then they went to bed. A couple of days later, they went to the secondhand store and bought a TV, couch, and dishes. Jewel loved looking through the store. There were so many interesting things, and they were so cheap.

Jewel got to pick out a wooden three-drawer dresser. It was white with purple flowers. She also got a twin bed and a table lamp. They rented a truck and took everything home and set it up. She loved her bedroom. She even had the twins over for a sleepover. Life couldn't have been any better.

Within a few months, the apartment was looking and feeling like a home. Nancy's cooking even started improving with help from the cookbook and some lessons with Mrs. Bridges. Jewel even got to go back to the secondhand store and get some pictures for her room. She got one of a sunrise and one of a beach. She had never been to the beach. Living in the middle of Iowa, there were no beaches around and no money for a vacation. She knew she would go to a beach someday.

Before she knew it, her twelfth birthday was coming up. Her mother told her she could have five friends come to the apartment for a party. She went to the store to get invitations, snacks, and decorations. It was the first birthday party she got to have at her house with friends. All of her other parties were at the Bridges house with just her parents and the twins.

Chapter 7

The twins were definitely coming, so she had to choose three more people. She thought long and hard before deciding. First, she chose Chole. She met her in second grade. She had long black hair and tan skin. Her dad was in the army, so he was gone a lot. Her mother was a homemaker. Next, she chose Heather. They were lab partners last year and became instant friends. They both liked chocolate ice cream and the color pink. Her last choice was Corey, a boy she had a crush on. He was tall with dirty-brown hair and brown eyes with gold flakes and an overbite. His dad is an electrician, and his mom a secretary. He had a younger sister in first grade. They were the typical middle-class family.

It was the morning of the party, and Jewel didn't sleep a wink the night before. She got up at eight in the morning on a Saturday. Her mother was at work and wouldn't get home till eleven, and her dad was sleeping from working the night before. Even though the party didn't start till one, she still had Steph to help her set up the decorations then waited for her mom to get home. On Nancy's way home, she picked up a cake and some ice cream. When she got home, she changed her clothes then helped Jewel get ready. Jewel had picked out a dark-blue dress with a white sash. Her mom braided her hair and let her put on some lipstick and eyeshadow. Jewel felt like a princess.

Soon, the guests started to arrive. They put on some music and danced around the living room, played some games, and drank punch. Finally, it was time for cake and presents. She opened the twins' gift first. They got her a new set of PJs with stars on them. Next, she got a dreamcatcher from Chole and a soccer ball from Heather. Last, she opened Corey's gift. It was a bracelet with a *J* on it. She said thank you to everyone, and their parents started to arrive to pick them up. When Corey's mom arrived, she gave him a hug, and he kissed her on the cheek. He said thanks for the party and left. Jewel just stood there holding her cheek. She felt like a woman for the first time. Nancy and Tony just looked at each other and shook their heads.

Chapter 8

When summer was over, Jewel was officially in middle school. In her town, the middle and high schools were in the same building. She didn't have much interaction with the older kids, except on the bus and in the lunchroom. It was a huge change for Jewel. A bigger school, more homework, and no recess. Jewel was really scared for her first day of school.

Nancy took her to the secondhand store to pick out some outfits for the first week. She also got her a new lunchbox and backpack. Nancy took off of work the morning of her first day of school, so she could help her get ready. Nancy got up early and made some French toast then put some pigtails in Jewel's hair. Soon, the bus was in front of her building. She kissed her mom goodbye and got on.

The first person she saw was Heather. They sat together the whole ride. When she got to school, the twins were waiting for her. They told her she had nothing to worry about then showed her and Heather around the school. They showed them where the bathrooms were and the lunchroom. Then took her to her first class. She gave them a hug and walked in. Her first class was history. When she walked in, she saw Corey. She was happy when the teacher sat them next to each other. Throughout the day, she found out that they had three classes together: history, math, and study hall.

Jewel was so happy when lunch came around. She sat with the twins and Heather. The twins showed them where all the different clicks sat. There were the jocks with the cheerleaders, the band geeks with the drama club, the science club with the math geniuses, and the goths with the slackers. Jewel wondered what group she would end up in.

When she got home, she told her parents all about her day; all the new rules, the teachers, and the lunchroom. She was so tired that she went to bed early. Within a few months, she knew her way around the school and had her schedule down. It was time for the first school dance, the Valentine's dance. She hoped so much that Corey would ask her. On Wednesday morning, Corey walked in with a handmade card that said, "Will you go to the dance with me?" She, of course, said yes.

On Friday night, she took a shower, and her mom curled her hair. Then she put on a red dress with sparkles and black flats. Corey came to pick her up with his dad. When she opened the door, Corey was wearing a black button-down shirt with a red tie. He was holding a single pink rose; Jewel blushed as she took it. She hugged her parents goodbye and left. At the dance, she drank some punch and danced with her friends. Then a slow song came on. Corey put his hands on her waist, and they both giggled. When the song was over, they went home, and she told her mother all about the dance. That night, she dreamt of her and Corey's wedding.

Before she knew it, it was spring break. She got home on the last day of school, and her parents were sitting at the table. They asked her to sit down, and they said they had something to tell her. They said that they had been saving all of their money and got tickets for a waterpark a few hours away for her and the twins. They were going to leave in the morning, drive up there, spend the night in a hotel, go to the park the next day, sleep in the hotel, then drive back. Jewel was so excited that she started packing imminently.

The next morning, Mrs. Bridges pulled up to the apartment and Jewel and her mother got in and they started driving. Jewel had never been out of town. She loved all of the sights and signs. A couple of hours later, they stopped at a diner for lunch. They got to the hotel around five. They got one bedroom with two beds. The girls slept in one bed and the moms in the other. Their moms let them get room service for dinner. They got grilled cheese and ice cream sundaes. The next day, the girls got up early and put on their bathing suits. The water park was so big; they had slides, a kiddie pool, and a waterfall; they didn't even know where to start. The girls had a great day and met some cool people from all over the place. When the day was over, they went back to the hotel and fell fast asleep. When they got back to school, they told all their friends about the waterpark. Before Jewel knew it, her first year of middle school was over. She made it through. She finished with an eighty-seven average. Her parents were so proud of her and took her out to dinner to celebrate.

Chapter 9

Over the summer, she would hang out at the local pool and sit at the restaurant with her mom. She had her party at the local pool. She was thirteen, officially a teenager. It seems like overnight, she started to change. She started to grow breasts and get hair in unfamiliar places. Corey started to change too. He started growing facial hair, and his voice started to crack. When they went back to school, Corey started hanging out with a new crowd—a group of high schoolers that he met over the summer while cutting grass. It was a boy named Mike. He had a rough life; his dad was in and out of jail. And his girlfriend, Amber. Amber never knew her father; her mom had her when she was sixteen and cared more about partying than parenting. They would cut class and smoke behind the gym. Jewel wasn't sure about Corey's new friends, but she liked Corey, so she didn't say anything about them. Soon, Corey started skipping class with them and going to high school parties.

One day, during lunch, Jewel asked Corey if he wanted to get some pizza after school on Friday. He said yes. When they got to the pizzeria, Jewel expressed her concerns about his new friends. Corey defended them, saying that she didn't know them like he did and that they didn't treat him like a kid. Jewel told him that he was growing up too fast. Corey got mad and stormed out. When Jewel got home, her mother could see that she had been crying and asked what was wrong. She told her that she and Corey had a fight and she thinks she had lost Corey forever. Nancy told her that everyone has disagreements from time to time and to give Corey a few days to calm down. When Jewel got back to school on Monday morning, she looked for Corey but couldn't find him. She finally saw him at lunch. He was sitting with Mike and Amber. She walked over to their table and asked Corey if they could talk.

Mike said, "No. I heard what you said about us being a bad influence on Corey. I think you should leave."

Corey just sat there and didn't say a word. As Jewel turned to walk away, Corey slipped a note in her hand. When she got back to her table, she opened it, it read:

Dear Jewel,

I'm sorry I stormed out of the pizza shop the other day. I know you don't understand my choices right now. But right now, I need to learn on my own.

I should have told you sooner, but my parents decided to get divorced over the summer. So I am really confused and scared right now. Feeling like an adult and being in control of my life is what I need right now to get through this. I hope you will wait for me to get through this phase of my life. If you can't and this is too much for you, I will understand. But I hope you will still be here when this is all over.

Love, Corey

That was the first time Corey had told her that he loved her, and she was happy. She knew she had to do what she could to support her friend in his time of need. So in study hall, Jewel wrote a note back to him. It said:

> Dear Corey,
>
> I am sorry to hear about your parents. If you need anything, let me know. I will always be here for you. I didn't mean to upset you at the pizza shop. I just don't want to see you get in trouble or hurt. If you ever need to talk, I am here.
>
> Love, Jewel

She passed him the note after class. He smiled when he took it. Jewel knew that they would be okay. That night at dinner, Jewel told her mother that she and Corey made up.

Nancy said, "I knew you would. Everyone fights, even me and your father, but if you care enough about each other, you will find a way to work it out and makeup."

As Jewel fell asleep that night, she wondered what would happen if her parents broke up. Who she would live with, how she would feel. She didn't get much sleep that night. Over the next few months, she started seeing less and less of Corey. But he would still put a note in her locker once a week, letting her know that he was okay and updates on his parents' divorce. Jewel got some pamphlets from Steph on teen drinking and slipped them in his locker. Corey's notes said that his mom cheated with someone at work and that she kicked his dad out of the house. As a result, his dad started drinking a lot. They started fighting about where the kids would live and who gets the cars and house. By the time summer came around, it had reached a boiling point. They were calling the cops on each other and couldn't be in the same room without getting in a screaming match.

One night in June, Jewel was sitting on the couch, watching TV, when there was a knock on the door. It was around nine at night, and it was pouring rain. She opened the door, and it was Corey, he was soaked from head to toe. He said that Mike and Amber left him at a party, so he started walking. He didn't want to go to either of his parents' houses and thought of her. Her dad was at work, and her mom was out with some friends; she knew she would get in trouble if she let him in but did anyway. She closed the door behind him and said she would get him some dry clothes from her dad's closet. When she came back, Corey was standing in the living room naked. Jewel was taken back for a second. It was the first time she had seen a boy naked. She walked over to him and handed him the clothes. He said thank you and told her that he really appreciated her being there for him through this tough time. Then he dropped the clothes and kissed her. She resisted at first then kissed him back. Before she knew it, they were on the couch making out. Then Corey took off her shirt and unbuttoned her pants. Jewel's heart was pounding so fast. Corey touched her cheek and told her that he loved her and asked her if she was okay. She took a breath and said yes and took off her bra. Corey's eyes skimmed her body and said, "You are so beautiful." They were on the couch with their hands all over each other's bodies. Jewel laid down with Corey on top of her, softly kissing her neck and working his way down her body. When he got to her underwear, Jewel touched his head and said she wasn't ready for that. Corey said he understood, and they got dressed and had some ice cream. They sat on her bed and talked till they fell asleep.

When Nancy got home around eleven, she went to check on Jewel and saw Corey in her bed. She turned on the light and asked what was going on. By now, everyone in town knew about his parents' divorce. Corey explained that he didn't want to go home, so he went there. He said he knew he should have left when he found out that her parents weren't home and took all the blame. Jewel jumped in, defending him. Nancy put her hand up and told them both to stop. She sat them both on the couch and called Corey's mom. Then she told them that she is happy that they have a strong friendship and can be there for each other and that they will need that to get through life. Then Nancy spotted Jewel's bra on the couch. The kids saw it and turned red. Nancy talked to them about sex and that it may feel good at the time, but it won't get rid of the pain and that they would regret it later. That it needed to be with someone you truly love and fully trust; also, they were too young. She felt like a hypocrite because of her previous job but knew more than anyone that she was speaking the truth. When their talk was over, she gave Corey a blanket and left him on the couch and told Jewel to go to her bedroom. Jewel told her mother that they didn't have sex, that she wasn't ready for that. Nancy told her not to let anyone pressure her, then tucked her into bed.

Once they were both asleep, she called Tony and told him what happened. He was mad at first, but Nancy calmed him down. They worried about her growing up too fast because of what she had seen in her life. When Tony got home in the morning, he talked to the kids about drugs, peer pressure, and how to put a condom on, hoping that they wouldn't have to use one for a while. Then they ate breakfast, and Nancy and Jewel took Corey home.

Chapter 10

Jewel didn't see Corey for the rest of the summer. He was grounded for sleeping over at her house. So on the first day of eight grade, she couldn't wait to see him. She spotted him as soon as she got off the bus. She ran up to him and hugged him. He kissed her and said he had so much to tell her. First, his parents stopped fighting and got the divorce settled because his mom got pregnant from her coworker that she cheated with. Corey moved into an apartment with his dad, only two blocks away from her apartment and that his dad had stopped drinking. His sister stayed with his mom. Then the bell rang.

Jewel couldn't wait till lunch so she could talk to Corey about that night in her apartment. Were they a couple or was it just a one-time thing? She was so confused. When lunch came around, she asked him if they could sit at a corner table to talk. Once they sat down, she asked him about that night, and he said that he had been thinking about it too. They both agreed that they had fun but moved way too fast. Then Corey asked her to be his girlfriend. She imminently said yes and gave him a peck on the lips. Soon the bell rang, and he walked her to class.

When Jewel got home that day, she told her mom about everything. Nancy was happy for her, but inside, she was still worried about her moving too fast because of what she has seen in her life. Over the next few weeks, Corey would walk her to class, carry her books, and hold her hand in the halls. They were the "it" couple of the eighth grade. Jewel liked all the attention, especially since she didn't see the twins that often. They were in high school now and busy with sports and clubs. The girls made an agreement that one Saturday a month, they would have a sleepover and catch up. At their first sleepover of the year, Jewel told them about her relationship with Corey and what happened over the summer. Lily had sex over the summer at camp. While Maddy was shy and never even been on a date. Lily did tell Jewel that her mom was right about moving too fast.

Lily did it with a boy named Bobby. He was sixteen and lived in New York City. It was the last night of camp, and they had been flirting for the last three weeks. They were the last ones at the bonfire that night. Bobby leaned over and kissed her. Then he asked her if she wanted to take a walk, she said yes. They walked down to the lake, and Bobby suggested they go skinny dipping. Lily was nervous but agreed. When they were done swimming, they got out and started getting their clothes. Bobby grabbed her and kissed her. They laid down on the dock and started making out. Lily told him that she had never had sex before and wasn't sure she was ready. Bobby told her that he had done it before and that it wasn't as big of a deal as people made it out to be and that if she liked him, she would show him. She still wasn't sure but went along with it because she did like him. She said that it hurt a little bit but only lasted about ten minutes. When they were done, they got dressed and went to their cabins. He took her number and promised to call her but never did. She didn't regret it but learned a valuable lesson about being more careful about who she gives her heart and body to.

Jewel knew it would be different with her and Corey. They grew up together and knew everything about each other. When and if they got to that point, Jewel secretly hoped they would but not just yet, they were only fourteen.

By the girls' next sleepover, Lily was dating a sophomore named Nick. He was on the football team, and she was a cheerleader, so they were the perfect couple. Jewel and Lily spent the night trying to convince Maddy to get a boyfriend so they could all go on dates together and have babies together when they got older, of course. But Maddy was a science nerd who wanted to become a doctor or find a cure for cancer. She was more interested in books than boys at the time. A few years later, they found out that she didn't care about boys at all.

Chapter 11

Two weeks later, Nick got his license and wanted to take Lily on a popper date to celebrate. She asked if Jewel and Corey could come and he said yes. It was the night of the double date, and Jewel was nervous because she had never been on a real date before. She tried on everything in her closet before she decided on a floor-length, light-blue skirt with a slit on the side to her knee and a white V-neck shirt with sparkles on the collar. She put on a pair of white sandals. Then she painted her fingers and toenails dark blue.

Her mom did her hair and makeup. Then her dad reminded her about peer pressure. She told him not to worry, but he put a condom in her purse anyway. Soon, there was a knock at the door. It was Corey; he had on a dark-green polo shirt and khaki pants. He bought a bouquet of flowers. She said thank you. Nancy took the flowers and put them in some water. Then she said goodbye and left. Nick and Lily were already downstairs, in the car. Corey opened the door, and they both got in the back seat. Nick had on a pair of dark jeans and a red button-down shirt. Lily was wearing a purple spaghetti-strap dress with black heels and red lipstick. They went to a local buffet for dinner. When they were done eating, the girls went to the bathroom as the guys paid. The girls talked about how grown up they felt and complimented about each other's outfit. Then they touched up their makeup and left. Next, they went to the movies. The four of them decided on a comedy. Then Corey got a small popcorn for them to split and two small sodas. Halfway through the movie, Nick and Lily started making out. Jewel and Corey moved over a

few seats and finished watching the movie.
When the movie was over, Nick took them
home. He dropped Lily off first.

Corey and Jewel waited in the car as he
walked her to the door. Then they took Jewel
home. Corey walked her to the door. Jewel
said thank you for dinner and a great night.
Then Corey kissed her and stuck his tongue
in her mouth. She liked it and started kissing him back. They were leaning on the door
when Tony opened it and they both fell back-
wards and on to the floor. Corey jumped up
and ran down the stairs. Tony stared at her as
she got up and went to her room.

The next morning, Nancy talked to
her about teenage pregnancy. And had Steph
bring over some pictures of STDs and talk to
her about labor. Jewel told them she wasn't
ready for sex, but they still wanted her pre-
pared. After that night, Jewel and Corey
became inseparable. They would sneak away

during lunch to make out and then they would go to Corey's house after school. They had two hours before his dad got home. About two months later, they were in Corey's bedroom, making out, when Corey slipped his hand in her pants. Jewel stopped him and said they needed to talk. She said she loved him and liked kissing but didn't want to do any more than that. Corey was confused. He stated that they had gone farther before; they had seen each other naked. Also, they had condoms, so why not use them. They understood about safe sex, not to get pregnant, and they were both virgins, so they didn't have to worry about STDs. He made a compelling argument. But Jewel was still unsure; she said that it was a big step, once you do it, you can't take it back. Corey got upset. He didn't understand why she didn't want to share this special milestone with him. She tried explaining that she did, just not right now, but he wasn't listening and kicked her out of the house.

She was bawling by the time she got home. Her parents asked her what was wrong, and she told them. Tony started asking her if Corey made her do something she didn't want to and what he would do to him if he did. Nancy jumped in and said she is so proud of Jewel for speaking her mind and not giving into peer pressure. Then Tony left for work. Jewel went down to the corner store and got some ice cream and candy. It was a Friday night, so Nancy let her stay up late and watch movies.

The next morning, she walked over to Corey's house, but he refused to talk to her. She spent the rest of the weekend in her room. On Monday morning, Jewel looked for Corey before class but couldn't find him. When she saw him at lunch, she asked him if they were okay, and he said he didn't know.

He said he was really upset that she didn't want to take the next step in their relationship. That he felt like maybe their relationship wasn't as strong as they used to be, that maybe she didn't care about him as much as he cared about her. She tried to protest that she loved him and that he had it all wrong. She just thought they were a little too young for sex. Corey brought up the point that neither of them had the best childhood, so they were mentally older than their physical age. By this point, they were in a screaming match and everyone in the lunchroom was listening. Then Corey said something that shocked everyone. Corey said that if Jewel didn't agree to have sex with him after school today, that they were done, and he would find a girl who wasn't afraid to show her love. Then he added that he couldn't understand how the daughter of a hooker could turn out to be a saint. Jewel slapped him across the face and said, "We are done!" And walked out of the lunchroom.

As soon as she was out of sight, she ran into the bathroom and started to cry. Lily came into the bathroom a minute later. Nick was in the lunchroom and texted Lilly the whole thing. Lilly told her everything was going to be okay and called her mom to pick her up. When her mom got there, she told her that boys could be dumb and think with their little head instead of the big one. That guys don't always think before they talk. Jewel asked if guys get better as they get older. Nancy laughed and said no. But that women get better at understanding what men are trying to say even if it comes out right and to know when they are thinking with the wrong head and just to ignore them. Jewel asked how she will learn all this. Nancy said that she learns from experience and intuition. She said that men don't get intrusion. Jewel asked what that was. Nancy said that it was the little voice in the back of your head that tells you when something doesn't feel right or alert you of danger. Then she added that, sometimes, you have to kiss a lot of frogs to find your prince. Then they pulled up to the secondhand store for some shopping therapy and went to the grocery store to get her favorite meal for dinner. When they got home, Tony asked what was going on and they told him. Tony got mad and wanted to go over to Corey's house, but Nancy told him violence isn't the answer and not to stoop to his level. Tony agreed and calmed down. That weekend, the three girls had a sleepover and burned everything Corey had ever given her.

Chapter 12

Over the next few weeks, there were a lot of whispers and rumors around school about that day in the lunchroom. Jewel did her best to ignore them and focus on her schoolwork. She would see Corey in the hallway and smile, but he would just look the other way and keep walking. She missed his friendship more than anything. The week before Christmas, she spotted Corey next to Sydney's locker. Sydney was a trust-fund baby who hit puberty early and everyone noticed. There was a rumor that she dated a tenth grader last year. She was a snob, and Jewel didn't understand what Corey was doing over there until Sydney walked up to him and kissed him. Jewel was shocked. She walked up to them and asked what was going on.

Corey said that he needed a girl that appreciates him and Sydney didn't mind showing him how she felt. Then Syd started chanting, "Jewel the nun," and got the whole hallway to join in. Jewel ran out of the hall. When she got home from school, she told her mom what happened. Nancy told her not to listen to the kids at school, to stand by her morals and be proud of them.

That Sydney may get all the boys now, but no one will want her as a wife when she gets older. That real men don't want a girl who has been with so many guys and is a stuck-up. Jewel wanted to get back at them but didn't know how. At her sleepover with the twins that weekend, she asked them to help her get revenge. Maddy suggested pranks, like super glue their butts to a chair or put drugs in their lockers. Jewel thought they were good ideas, but she was thinking something more personal. Lilly thought that, first, she needed a makeover then she needed to get a new boyfriend to flaunt her around school and show Corey what he lost. Jewel was a little unsure about the plan, she didn't like any of the other boys in class. So Lilly called up Nick and found that he had a friend named Adam who was new to school and didn't have many friends. Nick said he was from a good church family and would be a perfect gentleman.

Nick and Adam came over on Sunday after church and took the girls to the park. Adam was just as Nick described him. They spent the afternoon hanging out. Within a few hours, Jewel realized that she liked him as a friend and there was no spark. Adam felt the same way but agreed to pretend to be her boyfriend. But he made it clear that he doesn't believe in revenge and that he will do it to help out a friend. They came up with a plan that Adam would pick her up for school tomorrow, walk in, holding her hand, and have lunch together.

As soon as they got home from the park, the twins started on her makeover. First thing they wanted to do was cut her hair. Jewel said no at first, her hair was halfway down her back. The twins reminded her that this was a fresh start for her and that it would grow back. They called Nancy for permission and she said yes. Jewel sat down on a kitchen chair and took a deep breath as Maddy started chopping. They gave her a bob with slanted bangs, shaped her eyebrows, and put on some press-on nails. Then the girls and Mrs. Bridges took her shopping for some more grown-up clothes. They picked out some miniskirts, low-rise jeans, and heels. When the twins were done with her, she barely recognized herself. She felt and looked fierce, confident, like she was untouchable. Lilly helped her pick out an outfit for the next day. They decided on a pair of dark jeans, a purple off-the-shoulder sweater, and a pair of black pumps. Then they took her home.

Nancy told her how great she looked while Tony's jaw dropped to the floor. When he got over the shock, he asked her if she did this for Corey and that she should never change to make someone like her. She confessed that first, it was about Corey but then she told him about the boost of confidence she got and that was enough for Tony. The next morning, she got up early and took a shower. Then she put on some mascara and lipstick. Soon, it was time for school, and Adam was at her door. When they got to school, Adam grabbed her hand and they walked in. All eyes were on her. Then they spotted Corey and Sydney. Jewel's heart was pounding but you couldn't tell by looking at her. When Corey saw her, his eyes widened, and his jaw dropped. Jewel said hi and introduced Adam. Sydney put her nose up in the air and said a haircut doesn't change the fact that you can't satisfy a man. Adam jumped in and said that she satisfies him just fine, that he loves how spontaneous and romantic she was. Then he grabbed her butt and walked her to class.

She was the talk of the school. All day, people complimented about her hair and nails. At lunch, Jewel, Adam, and Nick sat together. She told them how nervous she was that morning, and Adam confessed that he made it all up on the spot. Then he apologized for touching her butt without permission; she said it was okay. All three of them couldn't help but notice that Corey couldn't stop staring and all the dirty looks from Sydney and her group of girls.

After school, she ran into Stephine in the hallway. Steph told her how great she looked and asked her if she and her parents wanted to come over for dinner to meet her boyfriend. Jewel said yes and had a great night. Her boyfriend was sweet, funny, and kind.

Over the next couple of months, Jewel and Adam became great friends. Jewel learned that he wanted to become a musician and played guitar in the church choir. His dad was a pastor, and he was the middle child of five. They moved there because his dad took over the local church after the last pastor retired. Jewel started going to church with him and learned a lot about God. Jewel convinced her parents to go. Tony tried it, but it wasn't for him. Nancy really liked it and even thought about getting baptized.

Meanwhile at school, they kept up the act. While Jewel and Adam were only pretending to be all hot and heavy at school, things were heating up with Nick and Lilly. One day, shortly before spring break, they were caught in Nick's car in the school parking lot. They got detention at school and grounded and got a long talk at home. Jewel spent spring break working on a science project with help from Maddy. She got a ninety-seven on it.

When break was over, the eighth graders got to pick their classes for the next year. They had the four main classes, gym, and got to pick two more classes. Jewel picked an art class and a health class. Corey and Sydney seemed head over heels in love with each other. They were constantly kissing in the hallway, and Corey was always bringing her gifts and flowers. Jewel acted like it didn't bother her but at night, when she was alone in bed, she would cry.

Soon, it was summer break. A week after school went out, Jewel was home alone, painting her nails, when there was a knock on the door. It was Corey. He said that

Sydney broke up with him and she was the first person he thought of. She reluctantly let him in and offered him a drink. They sat down at the table. He said he apologizes for what he said in the lunchroom and would do anything to take it back. Also, that Sydney was bossy and only cared about what he could buy her and his body. That they had nothing in common, and when he ran out of money, she dumped him. Corey said that he never stopped thinking about Jewel and liked the new look but hoped she didn't do it for him. Jewel said thank you and said that it wasn't for him. Corey admitted going all the way with Sydney and didn't see what all the hype was about. He said it only lasted a few minutes and he didn't feel any different afterwards. Then he said that he knows she is with Adam now and lost the best thing he ever had but hopes someday, they can be friends. As he got up to leave, Jewel grabbed his hand and told him to stay. He sat back down, and she told him that she only started dating Adam to make him jealous. Her and Adam decided to just be friends but kept up the act at school. Corey admitted that it worked. The first day he saw them together, he wanted to beat up Adam but knew it was his fault for losing her. Corey asked if there was any way she could forgive him for being so stupid. Jewel said that he really hurt her, and it would take some time. Corey understood. Then she hugged him and said that she missed him. They went and sat on the couch and talked for hours. Jewel asked Corey about sex, told him about Adam, and asked about his new baby brother. By the time Nancy got home from her double shift, they were on the couch giggling like no time had passed. She asked them what was going on. Jewel told her that Corey and Syd broke up and he came over to apologize to her and they just started talking and patched things up. Nancy said she was happy to see them friends again. Corey left and went home.

When Tony found out that they made up, he wasn't as happy. He was worried about Jewel getting hurt again. Tony let those feelings go quickly when he saw how happy Jewel was but still kept an eye on Corey. A couple days later, they went to the park and met up with Adam. At first, Adam was protective of Jewel but soon warmed up to Corey. When they were done, Adam drove them to Corey's house. When Adam drove away, Corey asked Jewel if she wanted to come up, his dad wouldn't be home for an hour. Jewel said no, so Corey went in to kiss her and she backed up.

Jewel said, "Just because I forgave you, doesn't mean we are back together. It will take some time to trust you again."

Corey said he understood and went upstairs.

When Jewel got home, she ran into Stephanie in the hallway. Steph told her that her boyfriend proposed, and she wanted Jewel to be one of her bridesmaids. Jewel was so happy and imminently said yes. She started helping Steph with the wedding after school. She helped with the invitation and party favors. A few days later, Steph took Jewel to the dress shop for a fitting. There she met Stephanie's best friend and future sister-in-law, she was also a bridesmaid. They tried on a lot of dresses before they decided on a knee-length light-orange dress with a cap sleeve. Over the next month, she helped Steph with the cake and flowers. When she wasn't helping with the wedding, she was at the pool.

Meanwhile, Corey was doing everything possible to regain her trust. When he wasn't cutting grass, he was with her picking her flowers and writing her love notes. One day, they spotted Sydney at the pool. They walked up to her and said hi. She looked at them and scoffed. She said that Corey wasn't right for her, that she was just using him. Then she said that they belong with each other, both losers.

As they walked away, Sydney said, "I hope you enjoy my sloppy seconds."

Chapter 13

It was finally the night before the wedding. Stephanie took Jewel to the hotel. The wedding was in the banquet hall. Jewel and the other bridesmaids were staying in one room and Stephine was in a room a few doors down. They made sure Stephanie had everything she needed for the next day. They got some room service then played around with some hairstyles for the next day. They decided on an updo for Stephanie and curls for the girls with baby's breath in their hair. Then they went to bed. They had to get up early the next day. The girls had breakfast then started getting ready. The wedding started at one. They all had to take showers, get hair and makeup done, then help Steph get ready.

Soon, Jewel went downstairs. The banquet hall was amazing. There were flowers everywhere and chandeliers on the ceiling. As she was admiring the room, someone came up behind her and grabbed her waist. She turned around and it was Corey. His father rented him a tux and he looked so handsome. He looked her up and down, and told her that she looked beautiful. Then Jewel went to get in line. She walked down the aisle with Stephanie's brother. When they got to the front, she turned around and the doors opened. Stephanie looked like a princess. She was wearing a ballgown dress with beading on the skirt. The ceremony was great, they wrote their own vows.

It was time for the reception. People made toasts and they cut the cake. Around three, while everyone was drinking and dancing, Jewel grabbed Corey's hand and took him upstairs to her hotel room. When they got inside, Corey asked what they were doing.

She said, "I'm ready."

He said, "Ready for what?"

She took off her dress.

He said, "Are you sure?"

Jewel said, "I love you." And started unbuttoning his shirt.

They got on the bed and started kissing. Corey took off his pants and started kissing her down her body. When he got to her underwear, he looked up at her. She smiled and nodded her head yes. He slipped them off then softly ran his fingers from her toes to her honey pot. He kissed her honey pot while she ran her fingers through his hair. He grabbed a condom and put it on. They both looked at each other and took a breath as they made love. When they were finished, they laid on the bed and cuddled for a few minutes before getting dressed. They got downstairs, just in time for Stephanie to throw the bouquet. Shortly after that, people started leaving.

Jewel's parents were at the wedding, so they drove them home. When they got to the house, Jewel said she was going to walk Corey home. On the walk home, Corey said that he never felt so close or trusted everyone as much as he did Jewel. That he knew what people meant my making love. They made love; he just had sex with Sydney. Jewel agreed and said that she hopes nothing changes between them. That she heard that sex can ruin a relationship. Corey grabbed her hand and looked her in the eyes.

He said, "Never. We connected like never before in that hotel room. We are meant to be together."

He kissed her and went upstairs.

Over the next week, they were both busy getting ready for school. They were high schoolers now. The night before school, Corey came over. They talked about high school, figured out what classes they had together, and started kissing. They decided only to go to second base.

Chapter 14

The next day, Jewel got up early and got ready. Her mom made her breakfast and took some pictures. Tony said he couldn't believe how grown up and beautiful she had become. Then she hugged her parents and left for school. She and Corey sat on the bus together. The first day was a blur. After about a week, Jewel had her schedule down and really liked her art class. Lilly tried to convince her to join the cheerleading team, but she said no. There was already so much new stuff going on, maybe next year.

Before she knew it, it was October. Every year, the high schoolers have a costume contest. They had the best individual, couple, and group. They decided to do a group costume with Nick and Lilly. Jewel was Little

Red Riding Hood; Nick, the lumberjack; Corey, the wolf; and Lilly, the grandma. Nancy took Jewel to the store for a red mini-skirt and a red t-shirt. Stephanie made her a cape. Lilly got some clothes from her grandmother and bought a wig.

It was finally Halloween, and Nick decided to pick them up so they could all walk in together. When she got downstairs, Corey was walking up the street and his eyes got wide. He said that she looked hot and that his wolf instincts were coming out. She said thank you and got in the car. They won first place and won a gift card to a fast-food place. When school was over, Corey and Jewel went to his house and reenacted how they thought the story should have ended.

Soon, it was Thanksgiving and Corey invited Jewel to his mom's house. She had a great time. She got to meet his little brother, hang out with his sister, and eat some great food.

When they got back to school, they saw Sydney in the hallway, and she had a black eye. They asked what happened, and she said it was no big deal, that she just tripped and fell. Over the next few weeks, they noticed more bruises on her and started to get worried. One day, Jewel walked in the bathroom and saw Sydney in one of the stalls crying. She asked her what was going on. Sydney said nothing and told her to go away.

Jewel just sat on the floor and said, "We may not be the best of friends, but I still care about you. And if someone is hurting you, I want to help if I can. No one has the right to put their hands on someone regardless of the reason."

Finally, Sydney took a breath and said it was her new boyfriend, he was in college. That he gets mean when he's drunk. Jewel asked why she doesn't call the cops or break up with him. Sydney said she loves him, and he feels bad afterwards. She said that he is getting help for his anger. Sydney made her promise that she wouldn't tell anyone. Jewel didn't want to, but she agreed.

That night at dinner, she asked her parents about domestic violence. They asked why. Jewel said they were learning about it in health class. They said it was a vicious cycle. First, something sets them off. It could be anything, they had a bad day at work, be jealous, or the dishes aren't done. They beat the victim. Once they have cooled down, they apologize and say it will never happen again. It just repeats itself over and over again. Jewel asked why the victims put up with it. They said that there are multiple reasons. Sometimes, they have no other place to go, low self-esteem, or the abuser threatens to hurt themselves it they leave.

Jewel didn't get much sleep that night. The next day, she tried to talk to Sydney. She told her what her parents said. Sydney refused to listen and said that he wasn't like the other abusers and that he was going to change. Jewel pleaded with her but got nowhere.

When Christmas break came around, Jewel had no idea what to get Corey. She didn't have much money. She decided on painting him a picture of his favorite baseball stadium and have Stephanie help her knit a winter hat. It was Christmas Eve and time for them to exchange gifts. Corey opened his first. He loved the picture and the hat fit perfectly. Then Jewel opened her gifts. First, she opened a beautiful scarf and some nail polish. When she was done, Corey pulled out a small box from behind his back. It was a silver bracelet with her birthstone in it. She smiled and kissed him.

When they went back after break, school flew by with midterms and projects. Before long, it was spring break. During spring break, she went to a fundraiser at Adam's church and won a basket full of bath stuff and hung out with Maddy and Lilly.

On the first day back at school, Jewel noticed that Sydney wasn't at school. When she didn't show up for a few days, Jewel started to get worried. She hoped her boyfriend didn't do anything to her. Her worst fears were realized on Thursday morning when the principal announced that Sydney was dead and that her funeral was on Sunday. All day on Friday, the teachers were talking about violence and there were extra counselors. But Jewel spent the day in a daze. She wondered if she had told someone, anyone about Sydney's boyfriend, then she would still be alive. At the time, she thought she was doing the right thing by not breaking her promise but now, she wasn't sure of anything. She went home on Friday night, and told her mom everything. Nancy told her that it is not her fault. That Sydney made her own choices. Even if Jewel had told somebody that, Sydney would have denied it or lied about how she got the bruises. Nancy said that she saw on the news that her boyfriend was put in jail. Jewel felt a little better knowing he would be punished for what he did. Jewel spent most of Saturday in her room just thinking about Sydney. Why she would allow a man to do that to her. It made her happy to know that she had Corey and that he would never hurt her.

After dinner that night, her mom helped her pick out an outfit for the funeral. Jewel had only ever been to one funeral. It was for the woman at the convenience store who used to watch her. Jewel was ten when she died and didn't fully understand what was going on. She knew that she died, and they got all dressed up and went to a church with a big box in the front of the church. But that was different, she was old and died of natural causes.

The next morning, she got dressed and her mom took her to the funeral home. She walked in and saw a lot of classmates crying. Then she spotted Sydney's dad next to the casket. Jewel walked up to him but when she went to speak, her mind went blank and her mouth got so dry. She started to panic when Sydney's dad looked at her and asked if she was a friend of Sydney's. She shook her head yes. He grabbed her and hugged her for what seemed like eternity, but Jewel didn't mind. When he let her go, she looked in the casket. Sydney looked like herself, just pale and sleeping. She had a scarf on to hide the cut on her neck. As she was standing there, Adam and Corey came up to the casket. Adam had them kneel and said a prayer. Soon, it was time to start. They sat and listened to family and friends tell stories about her. Jewel learned so much. When it was over, they went to the cemetery. Everyone threw a rose on the casket as it was lowered into the ground. Over the next week, everyone was pretty somber at school. They had extra counselors on hand for people to talk too.

By the time summer break came around, everything was back to normal. Over summer break, Corey got his permit. His parents bought him a used car for five hundred bucks. It wasn't much to look at. The paint was faded and chipped, it also had some rust, but Corey loved it. His father took him out for a driving lesson and Jewel went with them. He was bad. He kept slamming on the brakes and almost hit a parked car while turning. Finally, his dad said the lesson was over and drove them home. When they got there, his dad went upstairs with the keys. Corey asked Jewel how he did. She said that he could use some more practice and they both laughed. Then they made love in the back seat.

Over the summer, Jewel got a job with her mother at the diner. She would clean tables and sweep the floors. It wasn't glamour but it was a job. She saved all of her money and at the end of the summer, she went to the store and bought a vanity and some new clothes.

Chapter 15

School was back in session, and the twins were in eleventh grade and had to start thinking about college. Maddy had already picked out the top choices and was looking at scholarships. Lilly wasn't sure what she wanted to be. While Lilly was deciding, Jewel was taking more art classes. Her teacher thought she was really talented and convinced her to enter in a local art contest. They had to do a local landscape piece. Jewel decided to paint the trees at a local park. She loved the colors of the leaves with the season change. It was the night of the contest and her dad took off work so he could go. Jewel, her parents, and Corey got in the car and they left.

When they got there, all the paintings were on display and the judges were walking around looking at them. There were fifty paintings in the contest.

Jewel looked at some of the paintings and got nervous. She thought they were amazing and that she didn't have a chance of winning. Finally, the judges had made their decision. Jewel got third place. She got a ribbon and her painting along with the first and second place winners, pictures put on display in the local museum for the next month. Afterwards, her parents took them out for pizza to celebrate. On Monday morning, during announcements, they mentioned Jewel winning in the art contest. Then later that day in art class, her teacher gave her pamphlets for art schools. When she got home, she showed her mom. Nancy was so proud of her and said she could be the next Picasso. That night, they got a coffee can and any coins that Nancy got from tips would go in the can. They put a label on it that said, "college fund."

A month later, Jewel woke up feeling nauseous. She figured it was something she ate. She didn't think much of it until a few days later, when she realized that she hadn't gotten her period. As soon as Corey picked her up for school, he could tell something was wrong. She said they would talk at school. When they got to school, they sat on the bench. Jewel told him what was going on. Corey just turned white. Then Lilly and Nick walked up. They saw Corey's face and asked what was wrong. Corey just sat there frozen. Jewel started crying as she told them. Lilly hugged her and said everything was going to be okay. They came up with a plan that Nick would go get a test during study hall and she would take it during lunch and that there was no reason to freak out till there was a reason. The first half of the day seemed to drag. Finally, lunch came around and Lilly and Maddy met her in the bathroom. She took the test then had to wait six minutes for the results. While they were waiting, the twins told her that they would be there for her and help out however they can, but Jewel wasn't listening. She was thinking about her college plans going out the window and how her parents were barely making now. They couldn't afford a baby. Finally, the timer went off. The three girls looked at each other and took a breath as Jewel picked it up. There it was, that pink plus sign staring them in the face. Jewel just started crying. The girls hugged her and said everything would be okay. Then they went back to class. Jewel walked back in the lunchroom where Adam, Corey, and Nick were waiting. Corey looked at her and knew. He just put his head down on the table. Nick rubbed his back and said that it would be okay while Adam said a prayer with Jewel. After school, they went to Corey's house to figure out how to tell their parents. They decided just to get it over with like a Band-Aid. Corey called his dad and asked him to meet him at Jewel's house after work. As they were walking to Jewel's house, Corey grabbed her hand and said that no matter what, he will always be there for her. Even if he had to drop out of school and get a full-time job. He will do whatever he has to do to take care of his family. Jewel kissed him and said I love you. They got to the apartment building just as Corey's dad pulls up. He asked what's going on and they ask him to come upstairs. When they got upstairs, Jewel asked her parents to sit on the couch.

Corey squeezed Jewel's hand and said, "We have something to tell you."

Nancy said, "If you two want to get married, you should at least wait until you graduate. You can have a long engagement."

Jewel cut in and said, "That's not it."

Then Corey blurred out, "We're pregnant."

All three parents just went blank-faced. They sat for a long silence before Nancy asked about condoms. They said they used them every time, but it must have broken. Jewel started crying and asked her parents if they hate her. She knew they couldn't afford a baby and how important school was. They hugged her and said never, that they would figure it out. Corey's dad came out of shock and said that they would have to talk to his mother. He also said that they would help Jewel out with whatever she needed. Corey and his dad left to talk to his mom. His mother, on the other hand, wasn't as happy. She yelled at him for ruining his future and that they should put the baby up for adoption. Corey said that he loved Jewel and his baby. If she couldn't support his decision, then she didn't have to be part of their lives.

The next morning, Jewel asked Corey what his mom said. He said that she wasn't invited to the baby shower. Jewel gave him a hug. He smiled and said he was okay but she knew better. The two of them spent the weekend looking for jobs. They had decided that this was their baby and even though they are grateful for their parents' help, they needed to step up and do what they could for the baby.

A week later, Jewel went to the doctor. She had never been to a gynecologist before and was a little nervous. Corey went with her and her mom. She got in the room and put on a gown. After what seemed like an hour, there was a knock on the door. Walked in a lady in her forties with brown hair and brown eyes. Hi my name is Dr. Sue.

Jewel shyly said hi.

"I see you took a pregnancy test and it was positive."

Jewel said, "Yes."

"Well, let's take a look."

Jewel laid down and lifted up her gown. Dr. Sue put the gel on her belly and looked at the screen.

Then she pointed at the screen and said, "There." The three of them looked at a little ball on the screen.

Dr. Sue said, "It looks like you are about six weeks long."

Jewel got dressed as the nurse printed out the picture. Everyone was silent on the way home; it had finally hit them that this was real. When they got home, they showed Tony the picture. He started crying.

Jewel said, "Daddy, don't cry. I didn't mean for this to happen."

He said, "These are happy tears. When I was younger, I never thought I would live to be a grandfather. This also makes me think about your grandmother. I wish she could have been here to watch you grow up. But I know that she is watching you from heaven."

Jewel hugged him and said, "I know."

The next day at school, Jewel showed the twins the picture. They imminently started planning her baby shower. The teachers, on the other hand, weren't as pleased and asked her what her plan was. She said she was due in June, so she would finish the year, have the baby in the summer, and be back in the fall. The teachers were less than impressed with her plan. They asked her that what if she had to go on bed rest or the baby came early. She said that she didn't know and would figure it out. Along with the teachers grilling her, the halls were buzzing. People were whispering around every corner. Corey was getting high fives while Jewel was being slut-shamed. Corey stood up for her, but it didn't make a difference. People were going to think and say what they wanted no matter what.

When the day was over, Jewel was mentally and emotionally drained. She gets home and her mom asks what was wrong. She told her what happened and what the teachers said. She asked her mom what they would do if any of those scenarios happened.

Nancy said, "Let's just hope none of them do." When it comes to the other students. They have a small attention span and that something else will happen soon and she will no longer be the center of attention. Jewel agreed and went to bed.

Over the next few weeks, things settled down at school and Corey's mom came over to apologize. She said she may have overreacted and wanted to be part of the baby's life. Corey accepted her apology and was much happier to have his mom back. It was a week before Christmas and Jewel and Corey were at his house, talking about baby names. All of a sudden, Jewel got a sharp pain.

Chapter 16

Corey got worried and thought they should call someone. The pain went away in a few seconds; Jewel figured it was just the baby moving around. She told him not to worry and went back to looking at names. They decided on James for a boy and Michelle for a girl. Later that night, Jewel took a shower and went to bed like normal. Around midnight, Jewel woke up to a wet bed. She turned on the light and saw the bed covered in blood. She screamed for her mom. She told Jewel to get changed while she called a cab. They rushed to the hospital.

When the doctor came into the room, they told him that she was pregnant. The doctor got the ultrasound machine and moved it all around her belly.

Then he looked at her and said, "I'm sorry, you had a miscarriage."

She looked at her mom and broke into tears. The whole way home, she wondered if it was something she did or didn't do that caused it. Her mom assured her that miscarriages were common in teenage pregnancies and that nothing she did caused it. They got home just as Tony got home from work. He asked what was going on. Jewel started crying again as Nancy told him what happened. Tony just hugged her and said that everything was going to be okay. Jewel said she was going to go to Corey's house. Her parents said it's only seven in the morning and she should wait a couple hours. Jewel said she needed to see him now and started walking. She got to the house and knocked on the door. His dad opened the door, he asked if everything was okay and said Corey was still asleep. She asked if she could wake him up. He could tell that she had been crying, so he said yes and went back to getting ready for work.

She went into his room and saw him sleeping peacefully. She kissed him on the forehead, and he opened his eyes. He was startled to see her and sat right up and asked what was going on. She told him that she lost the baby and he started crying. His dad heard him crying and came into the room.

They told him what happened, and he said, "I am so sorry but God always has a plan and you need to find the silver lining. You may not see it now, but there is always a rainbow after the storm." He said when they get older and are ready, they can try again. Then he left for work. Jewel spent the rest of the weekend lying in bed, thinking about what the baby would have been like if it grew up. Her mom reminded her of what Corey's dad said. Someone up in heaven knew that they weren't ready for a baby. And as hard as it is to think about, she can go back to being a normal teenager and go to art school. When she gets older and more stable, she can try again.

Jewel understood and agreed with what her mom was saying but it didn't take away the pain she was feeling at the moment.

Chapter 17

When they went back to school after Christmas break, Jewel was feeling a lot better, physically and mentally. She hadn't seen or talked to the twins all break, so as soon as she saw them, she got teary eyed. She told them what happened, and they hugged her and said how sorry they were. By lunchtime, the whole school knew about her miscarriage. Some felt sorry for her while others spread rumors about how she killed the baby. When she walked in the lunchroom, Adam was there with a hug and a prayer for the baby.

By the time spring break came around, everyone had forgotten about her pregnancy and were talking about a girl who got a nose job. Jewel was happy to be out of the spotlight and back to her normal life. One day, over spring break, Jewel was hanging out at the twins' house when the mail came. Maddy had gotten a letter from her top school. She ripped open the envelope. She read it for a second and started jumping up and down. They asked what was going on, and she said she got accepted. They were so excited for her. As soon as their parents got home, she showed them the letter. They were so happy and took the girls out to dinner to celebrate. Lilly, on the other hand, hadn't started applying to colleges or had a clue what she wanted to be. Her parents told her she needed to start getting serious about her future. Even if she didn't know what she wanted to major in, she could apply to community college to do her core classes and always transfer later. She agreed and applied the next week.

Soon, school was out for the summer, and Nancy asked her if she wanted a big party for her sweet sixteen. She thought for a moment about everything that had happened over the last year and said no.

She said, "I want a small party here with my true friends. Just some pizza and cake."

Nancy asked, "Who are your true friends?"

Jewel said, "The twins, Corey, Nick, Adam, Stephanie and her husband."

The night before the party, the twins slept over. They spent the night talking about their future and how after college, they were all going to get an apartment together. That's if none of them are married yet, even if they were, they would all live in the same building to be close to each other. Also, moving somewhere warmer, like Florida or California. The next morning, the girls got up, ate breakfast, and decorated the apartment. Jewel took a shower and Maddy braided her hair. Soon people started arriving. Once everyone was there, they ate some pizza and opened presents. The twins bought her a new outfit.

Adam got her a journal. Nick gave her a gift card. Steph got some makeup, and her parents gave her art supplies.

Finally, it was Corey's turn. He pulled a small box out of his pocket. Jewel took the box and lifted the top, it was a silver ring with a pearl in the middle. Corey said that it was a promise ring; that when they turn eighteen, he will give her an engagement ring. He said he wished they were older now so that they could get married now, but for now, he was happy to call her his girlfriend. That they had to be soulmates, and he can't wait to call her his wife and come home to her every night. Tony told him to slow down, that they still have a few years till that happens.

Corey laughed and said, "I know."

Nancy hugged him and said she would be happy to call him her son-in-law in a couple years of course. Jewel said she loved it and agreed that they were soulmates. Nick and

Adam took the twins home. Jewel walked Corey home. They held hands the whole way there and talked about what they wanted at the wedding. When they got to the house, they showed his dad the ring but assured him that they could wait to get married. He smiled and said they make a great couple.

Jewel spent the rest of the summer working at the diner with her mom. Every dime she makes goes in the jar. By the end of the summer, she had three hundred dollars. They opened a savings account and put the money in it. The twins, Nick, and Adam were all seniors this year. They were all busy with senior activities and trying to get scholarships. Jewel only saw them at lunch and on the weekends, but it was okay because she knew they had to get their futures in order. Adam got into a music school two hours away. Nick got a football scholarship in the next state over. Lilly applied to the school Nick was going to but didn't get in. Nick assured her that they would still be together. He said he would come home on holidays and that she could come and visit him, but Lilly didn't like that. They got in a big fight. They finally made up a week later. They decided that they would figure out a way to make it work.

Jewel asked Corey what his plans were, and he said he wanted to get into advertising. They figured out that one of the colleges that he applied to was only a half hour away from one of the art schools Jewel was looking at. They figured that if they both got in, then they could get an apartment in the middle of the two schools.

Soon, it was Halloween, and they all went to a party at Nick's house. Jewel had never been to his house before. It was a huge five-bedroom, two-bath house. The party was held in the finished basement. His parents were cool and stayed upstairs. They listened to music and played truth or dare. It was a great night.

The next day was Sunday, and Jewel slept in since she was out late at the party. She was sitting on the couch, eating some cereal when her mom came in the door. She looked pale and her eyes were bloodshot. Jewel jumped up and asked what was wrong and why she was home so early. Tony heard the commotion and came out of the bedroom.

Nancy sat down at the table and told them that there was a grease fire, everyone got out okay, but the building was destroyed. The owner was old and probably wouldn't want to rebuild. Nancy started talking about money. Tony told her not to worry about money, that all that matters is that she is safe. He said he would pick up some extra shifts until she found another job. Later that night, they showed the diner on the news. There was a pile of steel and bricks where a beautiful building used to be.

Chapter 18

The next day, Nancy started putting applications in. Two months later, she still didn't have a job and Tony was exhausted from working double shifts. So Nancy went back to what she knew, back to the streets. Tony tried to talk her out of it, but her mind was made up. The first month was good. She got some of her regulars back. With Nancy back making money, Tony didn't have to work so much. They were both working nights, so they got to spend more time together. Everyone was happy.

Then one morning in February, Jewel woke up for school and her mom wasn't home yet. She figured she got a late customer and left for school. A couple hours later, she got called to the principal's office. When she walked in, Officer Bridges was standing there.

He told Jewel to come with him. She asked what was going on, but all he said was to get in the car. Then they drove to the hospital.

Her dad was standing out front with another officer. She got out of the car and asked him what was going on. He said he didn't know either. Officer Bridges took them to the elevator and pushed the button for the basement. Tony imminently looked at officer Bridges and said no. Officer Bridges just looked at the ground. Tony started crying. Jewel stood there, confused.

When the door opened, she saw a big sign that said morgue and suddenly understood. Mr. Bridges said that the trash collectors found her this morning next to a dumpster, and she was so badly beaten, they needed them to identify her. He said that she had only been there an hour or two when she was found. They walked over to the window and looked. Jewel knew right away that it was her. She fell to the floor and started bawling. Her father started yelling and cursing, wanting to know who did it. Officer Bridges said that they were still collecting evidence, but as soon as he knew something, he would tell them. The car ride home was silent.

After school, Corey came over to see why she left school. She told him and he was in shock. He didn't know what to say to her, he just held her. He called his dad and said he was staying the night. Corey spent the night just holding her and consoling her. Jewel didn't go to school the next day. She spent the day in her mom's bed, smelling her pillow and wearing her sweater to savor the last ounce of her scent.

That night, the Bridges came over with some food. The twins stayed the night with her. The next week was a blur. The funeral, the cops asking them questions, and constant people coming to the house with food and flowers. Jewel went back to school after two weeks. She was just going through the motions. The kids at school would either avoid her or give her looks of pity. Tony called the police station every day for updates. After three weeks, they had no witnesses and the one print they found at the scene wasn't on file. But they said they would keep trying. That's when Tony decided to take matters in his own hands.

He went to the streets and started talking to his old contacts to find out what girls were working that night. The girls were more open to talk to him instead of the cops. It took two months for him to find out who her last client was. Tony gave the name to Officer Bridges. He checked him out but didn't have enough on him to get his fingerprints. Tony was infuriated. Officer Bridges told him to give them time to gather evidence. That sometimes justice takes time, but Tony wasn't listening.

It took Tony a week to find him and set up a date with one of Nancy's friends. The plan was simple. Tony would hide in the bathroom of the hotel room and wait for him to arrive. The night of the date, Jewel was sitting at the table doing homework when Tony came out of the bedroom. He sat at the table. He told her that he was going to get justice for her mother. Jewel told him to be careful, then he gave him a hug and left. The next morning, Jewel asked her dad if justice was served. Tony said that the man who killed her mother will never hurt anyone else again. It was the first day since her mother died that she had a glimpse of happiness. Her friends could see it on her face and happy to see her moving on. But it was short-lived.

A few days later, Officer Bridges was at the door. He said that they had found the body and told Tony that he was under arrest. Tony said it was worth it and gladly went with him. Jewel moved in with Stephanie during the trial. The Bridges offered for her to move in with them, but she wanted to stay close to Corey.

The trial was long, and when he was found guilty, Jewel's heart broke. She had mixed feelings. She felt like she lost her dad but knew what he did was right. He was sentenced the first week of summer break. After he was sentenced, Jewel had to decide where she was going to live permanently. She was at the apartment, packing her things, trying to decide where she wanted to live.

When Corey's dad came to the apartment, he offered for her to live with him with a few conditions. First, she had to get on birth control; second, she had to finish school; and third, she helps with chores around the house. He said that she is going to need Corey to get through this tough time and can see the twins anytime she wants. She agreed, and the paperwork was signed.

A month later, she spent her birthday with her dad at the prison. He told her that his lawyer was working on an appeal, and even if he lost, he could be out in fifteen years with good behavior. He said they would be together again soon.

Maddy went off to school, and Lilly stayed home and went to community college. The girls stayed close during her senior year.

Jewel went to see her father once a month. She told her father that she and Corey both got into the schools they wanted to go to, and she even got a scholarship. He told her how proud he was and how proud her mother would be. He lost his appeal but assured her that they would be back together soon.

On graduation day, she went and saw her father and told him that she and Corey got an apartment near their schools. She promised she would come to see him on school breaks and constantly call and write.

He wished her luck and told her not to worry about him, that this was her time to explore and show the world what she can do.

The next day, they packed up the car and said goodbye to Corey's dad. Then they went over to the Bridges house. Mr. and Mrs. Bridges gave them a gift card for food. Then Officer Bridges gave Jewel a bottle of pepper spray. The girls promised to keep in touch. Then they got in the car and started their new life together.

The end.

About the Author

Amanda was born on July 19, 1989, in Rochester, New York, to James and Michelle Vandervoort. She was raised around her loving parents, her stepmother, Sue, along with her five brothers and sisters. She graduated from Maryvale High School in 2007. When she was twenty years old, she married her best friend and the love of her life—John Schwartz—of Corfu, New York, with whom she had a daughter named Annalynn. She also was blessed with six beautiful stepchildren. She currently resides in San Angelo, Texas. She works as a certified nursing assistant in a nursing home. She loves her job but hopes to be a registered nurse someday. In her spare time, she loves to write, listen to music, and watch romantic comedies.

CPSIA information can be obtained
at www.ICGtesting.com
Printed in the USA
LVHW030112200721
693160LV00004B/586